THE NATURE COMPANY

UNDER THE SEA

In 3-D!

**Photographs and Text
by Rick and Susan Sammon**

**Starrhill Press
Washington, D.C.**

Dive In

Scuba divers are weightless underwater, just like astronauts in space. With scuba gear a diver can "fly" in any direction and experience all the wonders of the sea.

In our 15 years of scuba diving we've made more than 1,000 dives. We've explored waters all over the world, at every time of day and night. We've seen whale sharks as large as school buses and coral reefs filled with amazing colors. Each dive feels new, because there are always different and exciting things to see.

With our photographs we are able to share this marvelous undersea world with you. In this book are some of our newest three-dimensional (3-D) pictures. Wear the enclosed 3-D glasses and the pictures will come alive. You'll feel like you too are scuba diving.

In our travels we are sad to find pollution that destroys the places where sea creatures live. We are also unhappy when we see factory fishing boats and huge fish nets, which take more fish than can be used for food. The underwater world is a fragile ecosystem. We must learn to treat it with respect. If not, many marine species will become extinct.

We were careful not to disturb the animals, plants, and habitats we encountered while taking the photographs for this book. It is up to everyone to protect our oceans so creatures like these can always be a part of our world.

Rick and Susan Sammon

Croton-on-Hudson, New York

MORAY EELS

MORAY EELS may look like snakes, but they are fish. They breathe by opening and closing their mouths, so they almost always look scary and ready to bite. This spotted moray eel lives in the warm, shallow waters of the Caribbean Sea.

HABITAT
During the day moray eels hide in the cracks and crevices of coral reefs—or in the dark holds of a sunken ship. They tend to live in the same spot for a long time. Some morays share their homes with other eels, but most live alone. Like many marine animals they will fight to defend their territory.

PREY
Moray eels usually feed at night. They are swift predators who use their razor-sharp teeth to eat a variety of fishes, crabs, and octopuses.

PHYSICAL CHARACTERISTICS
Most fish have side and bottom fins, which help them swim. Moray eels do not. To swim they must swish their long bodies back and forth like snakes.

FUN FACT
Some eels grow as long as ten feet. Even at this size they are not much interested in attacking a diver.

SCUBA is an acronym for Self-Contained Underwater Breathing Apparatus. This system, sometimes called an aqua lung, was developed in the early 1940s by two Frenchmen, Jacques Cousteau and Emile Gagnan, and their basic design is still in use today.

Despite what you might think, scuba tanks are not filled with oxygen. They contain the same air we breathe normally, which is only about 17 percent oxygen. This is pumped into the tanks using an air compressor. At a depth of 60 feet, a diver with a full tank of air can stay underwater for about one hour.

A scuba mask puts a layer of air between a diver's eyes and the water. This lets the diver see clearly underwater. Near- and far-sighted scuba divers wear contact lenses or have special optical lenses attached to their masks.

Wet suits don't keep scuba divers dry. In fact, they are designed to leak just enough to maintain a thin layer of water between the diver and the suit. The diver's body heat warms up this layer of water, which keeps the diver relatively comfortable.

CHRISTMAS TREE WORMS look like

their name. Can you see why? It's a bit hard to believe that these colorful animals are cousins of the drab earthworm in your backyard.

HABITAT

Christmas tree worms make long tubes to live in on coral reefs. The worm's body is hidden in the tube. Only the beautiful gills, which trap floating plankton, can be seen by scuba divers.

DEFENSES

When a Christmas tree worm senses movement or a shadow, it can disappear into its tube in less than one second. Once inside the tube, the Christmas tree worm folds a tiny trap door over the tube's opening.

FUN FACT

Christmas tree worm is the animal's common name. Common names make it easier for nature buffs to identify animals. Besides, who could remember the Christmas tree worm's scientific name—*Spirobranchus giganteus giganteus*?

BIG EYES can see well in dark caves. Their large eyes help them find food and swim at night. But big eyes also have another way to get around in the dark. Like all fish, big eyes have a long line on the sides of their bodies that can detect even the slightest movement in the water.

HABITAT
During the day adult big eyes are found in small schools in dark caves. At night they leave the cave to look for small fishes and crabs to eat. Young big eyes live away from the reef and are very hard to find.

SCIENCE EXTRA
At dusk scuba divers can see nighttime fishes like big eyes leave their caves while daytime fishes come home to sleep. At dawn the day and night fishes switch places.

FUN FACT
An underwater flashlight helps a scuba diver see the true color of the big eye—dark red. But when big eyes are in dark caves, they look brown. This color makes it very hard for predators to see them.

SEA ANEMONES look like beautiful flowers,

but they are animals. Sea anemones are fierce predators. With their sticky tentacles, they can paralyze and trap fish. Some anemones are harmful to divers, but most are not.

HABITAT
Strong suction disks allow sea anemones to attach themselves to rocks. Anemones hardly ever move.

PREY
Anemones aren't picky about their food. They'll eat almost anything that floats into their tentacles, from microscopic sea animals to medium-size fish.

PHYSICAL CHARACTERISTICS
Some sea anemones have dozens of tentacles, others have more than two hundred. The tentacles are filled with water and flow gently in ocean currents. Anemones come in many colors—red, gray, green, pink, yellow, and brown.

FUN FACT
Certain species of clownfish, crabs, and cleaner shrimp live among the tentacles of the sea anemone. They don't feel the sea anemone's sting. Can you see the tiny shrimp in this picture?

SHARKS

SHARKS are very ferocious, or so people think. In fact, many of the 250 different species of sharks will avoid divers if possible. Still, like all wild animals, even the shyest sharks should be treated with respect and not teased.

HABITAT

Most sharks swim all day and all night. They must be on the move to pump water over their gills to get oxygen. If sharks stop swimming, they will sink.

BEHAVIOR

Some species of shark swim in schools of 100 or more animals. Others prefer to live alone or in pairs. If a shark is interested in a diver, the shark will circle the diver with its fins pointed down. This is the signal for the diver to get out of the water. The diver must be careful to move slowly. If the diver panics and thrashes about, the shark is more likely to attack.

PREY

Sharks will eat almost anything at any time of day or night. They usually go after bleeding or sick fish. A shark can smell one drop of blood in one million drops of water.

SEA CUCUMBERS are called the "vacuum cleaners of the sea." They spend their lives crawling on the sand, sucking up and eating small organisms as they move from spot to spot.

PHYSICAL CHARACTERISTICS

There are furry sea cucumbers, smooth sea cucumbers, and spiny sea cucumbers. Some are only ten inches, while others are six feet long. All look something like the cucumbers from a vegetable garden. Do you think this one does?

DEFENSES

A sea cucumber looks helpless, but it can be very tricky. When a crab or an eel comes prowling, a sea cucumber can stick out part of its stomach. This delicacy distracts the attacker. Another type of sea cucumber defense is to spit out long sticky tubes. The tubes trap the predator. Sea cucumbers then crawl away safely and grow either a new stomach part or new sticky tubes.

FUN FACT

Sea cucumbers have no eyes but are sensitive to light. If a diver swims over one, the shadow will make the sea cucumber seek shelter.

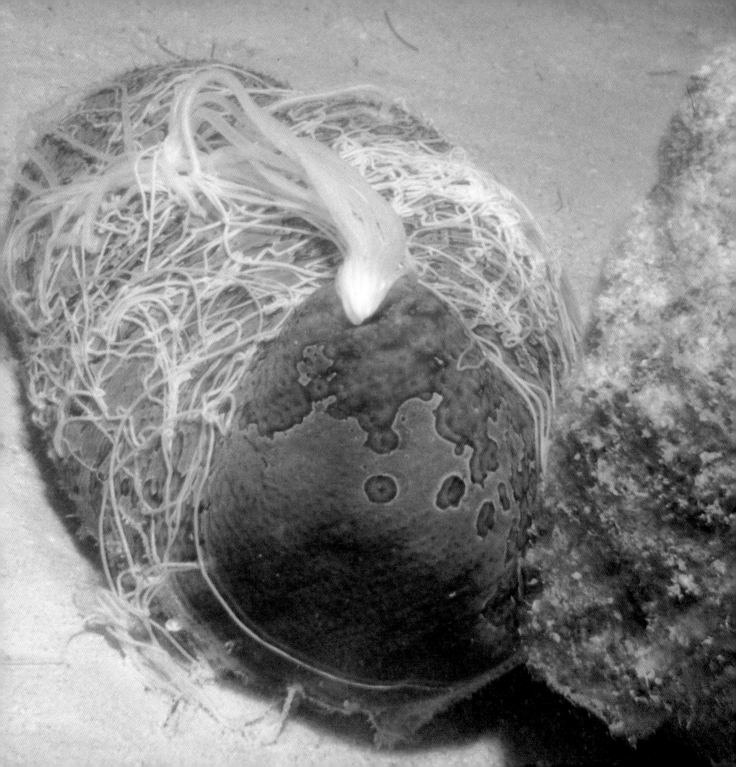

TRIGGERFISH are named for the small spine on their backs. The spine pops up like a trigger when the animal is frightened. The sharp spine warns a larger fish that if it catches a triggerfish, it will get a sharp poke in the mouth.

HABITAT
Most triggerfish are found in shallow water, but some live almost 100 feet below the waves.

PREY
Sea urchins, with their long, sharp spines, are the favorite food of triggerfish. With a powerful squirt of water, the triggerfish can flip the urchin over. Then, in a few quick bites, the triggerfish eats the inside of the urchin.

PHYSICAL CHARACTERISTICS
Triggerfish can change color to hide from predators. A queen triggerfish can be blue, yellow, and green one minute and almost white the next.

FUN FACT
The triggerfish in this picture is protecting its nest from nearby fish. If the triggerfish swims away, the other fish will eat its eggs.

OCTOPUSES are masters of camouflage. They change their color and shape to match the surrounding coral reef or rocks and can become almost invisible to predators and prey. When an octopus is threatened, it squirts out dark ink to confuse predators. Then the octopus can swim away to safety.

HABITAT

Octopuses often live in holes in the coral reef. But they also make their homes in sunken bottles, tires, and cans.

PREY

When some octopuses get hungry, they open their arms and drop like a parachute on a small coral head. This move traps all the animals in the coral. Then the octopuses use the ends of their arms to pull out breakfast, lunch, or dinner.

SCIENCE EXTRA

The octopus is related to other invertebrates such as squid, cuttlefish, and nautilus. The squid has nerves much like our own—only larger and easier to see. Scientists like to study squid nerves to gain a better understanding of the human body.

FUN FACT

An octopus has three hearts.

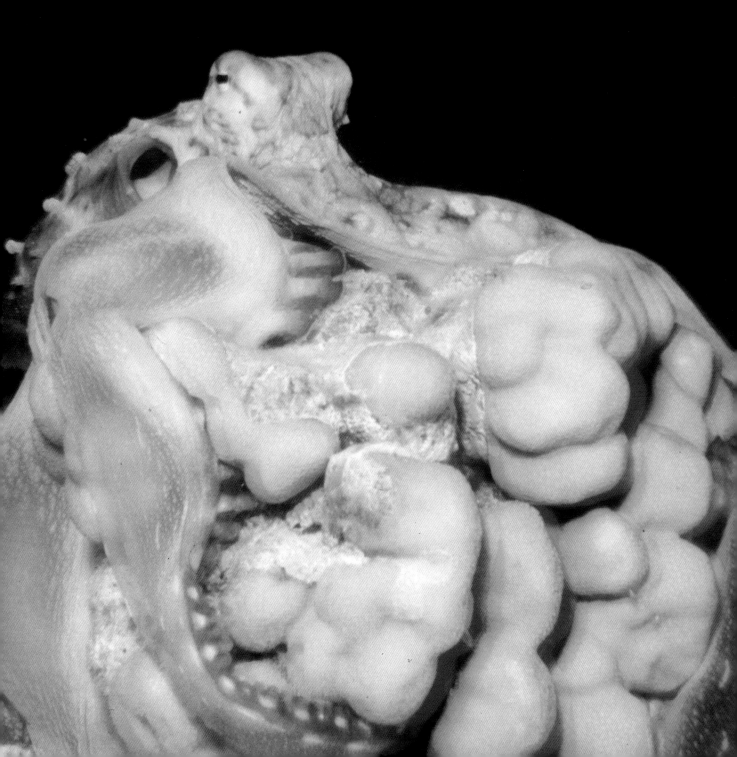

LONG-SPINED SEA URCHINS are

sometimes called the porcupines of the sea. If a diver brushes against one of their thin, sharp spines, it can break off and become embedded in the victim's skin. The spine's barb makes it impossible to remove—but fortunately it does dissolve harmlessly in a few days.

HABITAT
Sea urchins are bottom dwellers. During the day, they tuck themselves into crevices in the reef. At night, they move over the reef on tubelike feet, feeding mostly on algae.

SCIENCE EXTRA
Long-spined sea urchin eggs are considered a delicacy in some countries. As a result, these animals are heavily fished in certain areas. Where this has happened, algae has overgrown parts of the reef, killing coral and further upsetting the delicate balance of nature.

FUN FACT
All sea urchins have five sharp teeth, which they use to scrape algae from coral and rocks.

SCORPIONFISH can be a hazard to scuba divers.

If a diver accidentally steps on one, its sharp spines inject a painful venom into the diver's foot. The scorpionfish is named after the scorpion that lives in the desert, which has a poisonous stinger in its tail.

 ### HABITAT
Scorpionfish lie very still on the bottom of the sea and on coral reefs. If they sense a diver, scorpionfish will not move.

 ### PHYSICAL CHARACTERISTICS
Even expert divers find it very difficult to spot scorpionfish, because they look so much like rocks.

 ### PREY
Small fish also find it hard to see a scorpionfish. When it is hungry, the scorpionfish waits until a bite-size fish is near. Then the scorpionfish opens its mouth and sucks in the fish in a split second.

 ### SCIENCE EXTRA
Most fishes have a special balloon-like organ called a gas bladder that helps keep them afloat. The scorpionfish doesn't have a gas bladder, so it can't swim for too long. Most of the time it stays on the bottom of the sea.

MANINI

MANINI are very friendly. Scuba divers can reach out and touch them when exploring a coral reef. From a distance a school of manini looks like a large, yellow cloud floating over the reef. This type of swimming is called schooling. Predators think the school is one big fish instead of lots of little ones. Schooling discourages predators from attacking.

HABITAT
During the day manini are found in shallow water. At night the school breaks up and the individual animals disappear into deep cracks in the reef. These colorful fish are found in the Indian and Pacific oceans.

PREY
Swimming in schools of 50 or more fish, manini descend on a section of reef and eat small gardens of underwater plants.

FUN FACTS
On the reef manini live with about 400 different species of fish. Manini are also called convict fish because the stripes on their body look like the stripes on old-fashioned jail uniforms.

Behind the Scenes

Taking the 3-D pictures for this book was a thrill, but hard work as well. Just take a look at all the gear we needed.

SCUBA EQUIPMENT

Wet suit	Keeps us warm underwater.
Tank	Provides air, usually for one hour.
Regulator	Ensures an even flow of air.
Pressure gauge	Tells us how much air we have in our tanks.
Depth gauge	Shows us how deep we are diving.
Diving computer	Lets us know how long we can stay down at different depths.
Weight belt	Because wet suits make us float, we need these weights to help us sink.
Buoyancy compensator	Helps us become weightless underwater.
Mask	Allows us to see underwater.
Snorkel	Lets us breath while swimming on the surface.
Fins	Help us move faster underwater.

PHOTO GEAR

Customized close-up lens	For pictures of small creatures.
Custom-built 3-D camera	For pictures of schooling fish and shark.
Underwater housing	Built for customized 3-D camera.
Underwater strobe light	Adds light to underwater pictures.
Underwater flashlight	Helps us to see when diving at night.
Special underwater film	To record colorful underwater pictures.
Rechargeable battery	For underwater lights.
Battery charger	For charging batteries.
Tool kit	For fixing and adjusting cameras.

The pictures in this book were taken in Bonaire, Netherlands Antilles, and Tahiti, French Polynesia.